WEST SOMERSET VILLAGES

IN OLD PHOTOGRAPHS

FROM THE HOLE COLLECTION

THE SHOP FRONT, taken shortly after Herbert Hole had established his business in 1856.

HERBERT HENRY THE FIRST on his tricycle.

WALTER posing on his motorbike in the studio.

WEST SOMERSET VILLAGES
IN OLD PHOTOGRAPHS
FROM THE HOLE COLLECTION

COMPILED BY
KIT HOUGHTON AND LESLEY THOMAS

ALAN SUTTON

Alan Sutton Publishing Limited
Phoenix Mill · Far Thrupp · Stroud · Gloucestershire

First published 1991

British Library Cataloguing in Publication Data

West Somerset villages in old photographs.
I. Houghton, Kit II. Thomas, Lesley
942.385

ISBN 0-86299-947-2

Typeset in 9/10 Korinna.
Typesetting and origination by
Alan Sutton Publishing Limited.
Printed in Great Britain by
The Bath Press, Avon.

CONTENTS

INTRODUCTION

All the photographs contained in this book were taken by three generations of photographers who ran a small family business in Williton from 1856 until 1974.

The business was founded by Herbert Henry Hole when he was just twenty-one years old. After serving a seven-year apprenticeship with Flixton Golding Dowty, a printer and bookbinder in Bridgwater, Herbert managed to rent a premises at Long Street, Williton from the Wyndham Estate. The property at that time consisted of an eight-roomed house, with one of the front rooms converted into a shop (see photograph on p. 2) and outbuildings at the back which were used as printing workshops. Although initially a printing and bookbinding business, photography was becoming very popular, and it gradually began to absorb more and more of Herbert's time. He eventually built a large photograhic studio in the garden behind the premises and began advertising as a photographer: 'H.H. Hole begs to call the attention of the inhabitants of Williton and its neighbourhood, to his superior Ivory-toned Ambiotype Portraits, possessing all the delicacy of the Daguerreotype, without the usual metallic glare so much objected to; they do not fade and will bear washing like a piece of porcelain. N.B. Lessons given in Photography'. (Advertisement from the *West Somerset Free Press*, 3 November 1860)

Business flourished during the next few years and Herbert soon became well known in the district. He would fly a flag from a pole above his shop in Williton, indicating to people when he was 'in session'. He also published a kind of news-sheet, but when news was short he would make an announcement to that effect and suspend its publication until a more favourable time. His second wife, Charlotte, helped a great deal in the business, sensitizing the albumenized paper, printing and washing the photographs under a pump in the shed.

With business doing so well he decided to expand, and opened branches in Minehead and Watchet. His eldest son Frank took over the shop in Minehead. Herbert attended the 'Minehead Gallery' every Friday, the Watchet Studio on Mondays and Thursdays, and was at his Williton shop on Tuesdays and Wednesdays. He would commute between these premises on foot.

At the time of Herbert's death in 1900, Frank was still in charge of the Minehead branch, while his younger son Walter, was studying photography at Islington in London. He was called home in 1903 to take over the Williton end of the business from his mother, who had been carrying on as well as she could after her husband's death. But only eight years later Frank died, which resulted in a series of none-too-successful managers looking after the Minehead branch. Eventually

HENRY taking a photograph of his wife Muriel.

both that and the Watchet branch were closed, and all efforts concentrated once more at Williton.

During the First World War, Walter served as a photographer with the Royal Flying Corps and the RAF in France. He flew in the old R.E.8s and Bristol Fighters and went into Germany with the occupying army as a photographic instructor. In 1918 he was demobbed and came back to Williton to pick up the threads of the business again, which had suffered a great deal during the war with several large debts outstanding. However, with a lot of hard work he managed to pay off these debts and get the business back on its feet again.

The only transport Walter had at this time was a bicycle, and he would travel miles on different assignments, often carrying very heavy cameras and other studio equipment, before hurrying back to his darkroom to work well into the night so that he could produce his photographs before any of his rivals in the district. He took on an assistant, Mr Reg Branchflower, and as a sideline to the business the two men would put on magic lantern slide shows. They were soon in great demand, giving illustrated lectures – many of them had a religious background – with lantern slides using light produced from a carbide gas generator. These shows must have played a large part in the limited social life of the villages at that time.

As the market for local-view postcards opened up, Walter decided to go into production himself. He eventually managed to produce more than thirty thousand a year and distributed them all over West Somerset through wholesale agents, village post offices and stores. At the same time he was enlarging the shop and improving the studio, although he didn't actually buy the premises until the end of the First World War. It is believed that he paid the Wyndham Estate £400 for the property. His photographic work consisted mainly of family groups, portraits, weddings, and football and cricket groups.

As amateur photography became popular, he installed deep tanks for developing films and a printing machine. But when the chemists began a processing service for amateurs, Walter retorted by selling his films with stickers attached to them bearing the message: 'you don't send your watch to the blacksmith, so why send your photographic work to a chemist'.

During the 1930s he extended his property by building a second shop with a flat over the top. He bought a car, which must have made travelling around a lot easier, although there is no evidence that he went further afield.

Walter had married in 1917 and had a son (the second Herbert Henry) and a daughter. Henry – as he liked to be called – came into the business after leaving grammar school at the age of sixteen and began to learn the basics of his father's trade. When he was eighteen he was sent to Newton Abbot to train for a year before returning to Williton to assist in the business. At the outbreak of the Second World War he joined the RAF and was lucky enough to get a place at the school of photography in Farnborough. While there, he joined 35 Squadron RAF Bomber Command and was enlisted in aerial photographic work, some samples of which he still has in his family album.

During his time in the RAF Henry served in India and Northern Ceylon, finally returning home to Williton in 1946. But he had been home no more than four months when his father died unexpectedly from a stroke, and he was thrown in at the deep end of the business. With the help of his wife Muriel and a lot of hard work, he managed to increase the sale of postcards from twenty-five to thirty-three thousand a year between 1947 and 1949, and also to improve the business generally. The darkroom and studio were redesigned and new equipment installed. Business continued to improve and they were able to take on an apprentice, a Miss Powe, who quickly picked up the skills of printing, finishing and colouring. She stayed on for twelve years. During these years the business flourished and possibly reached its peak in 1952 when 1,050 photographs were taken, 31 weddings attended, 22,560 postcards printed, 86 children photographed and 1,209 amateur films developed!

Everything ran smoothly for nearly twenty years, but as he got older, Henry was becoming increasingly crippled with arthritis and was eventually forced to give up the business in 1974. The premises were sold to the Williton Radio and Television Company, and the stock and equipment was sold off to various buyers, thus ending 118 years of photography by three generations of one family.

While it is common today to find photographic studios in every town, the fact that a small village, such as Williton must have been then, possessed the facilities 'to have one's picture taken' must be regarded as remarkable, and a tribute to the initiative of the first Henry Hole. Photography at that time was still in its infancy (details of the first practicable method of photography were not revealed to the public until 19 August 1839) and Mr Hole was probably taking quite a chance in developing his business along such lines in a small village. However, it paid off and as the following pages demonstrate, he has left us with an invaluable record of West Somerset village life, dating back more than a century and providing us with a nostalgic glimpse into the past.

East of the Quantocks

AISHOLT. The fifteenth-century church lies on such a steep slope that the churchyard is almost level with the old belfry. Sir Henry Newbolt and his wife lived in a cottage here which Coleridge thought too lonely, and so moved to nearby Nether Stowey.

THE HIGH STREET, Cannington. This photograph was probably taken around 1935.

THE WAR MEMORIAL, Cannington. The large willow tree on the left was pulled down recently.

THE BLUE ANCHOR, Cannington, now renamed The Friendly Spirit because it is believed to be haunted.

EAST STREET, Cannington, showing Frog Cottage on the left.

THE MAIN ROAD through Cannington, showing Longstones Garage on the left and Loos Cottage next to it.

LONGSTONES GARAGE, Cannington, before the alterations.

CANNINGTON looking down East Street, showing Frog Cottage on the right. This photograph is believed to have been taken around 1935.

DODDINGTON HALL, with Escott Fewings in the foreground, one of two brothers who shared the Hall in the 1930s.

EAST QUANTOXHEAD. This village has been the home of the Luttrell family since the time of Domesday. The early historian Leyland wrote: 'I saw a fair park and Manor place of the Lutterelles caullid Quantock Hedde bycause it standeth at the heede of Quantock Hilles towards the se'.

THE BEACH at East Quantoxhead. I wonder if these three girls posed especially for Walter, or whether he took the photograph because he saw them sitting there.

A THATCHED COTTAGE at East Quantox-head which had been struck by lightning.

THE FOURTEENTH-CENTURY CHURCH at Fiddington has a fine Jacobean pulpit, medieval bell and the remains of an ancient cross.

CHURCH ROAD, Fiddington. The cottage on the right, which used to belong to Mr Hagget, has now been demolished.

HAWKRIDGE, near Spaxton, showing the road to Nether Stowey on the right.

LOOKING IN THE OPPOSITE DIRECTION at Hawkridge from the above photograph. The area in front of the road is now the site of a large reservoir.

ALFOXTON PARK HOTEL. near Holford. This is believed to be one of the earliest photographs taken of the Alfoxton Hotel, famed for its links with Wordsworth who moved there with his sister to be near his friend Samual Taylor Coleridge.

OLD BEECH TREES at Holford. They were locally known as the Alfoxton Beeches and have recently been pulled down.

THE MEET at Holford Bowling Green, c. 1935.

THE PLOUGH INN at Holford, showing Mr Browning's blacksmith's shop in the foreground.

ACCOMMODATION
COACHES INVITED.
GOOD PULL IN.
ON BRIDGWATER
MINEHEAD MAIN ROAD.
SKITTLE ALLEY.

16th CENTURY INN
HOST
F.V. GAUNTLETT

TEL. HOLFORD 232

'THE PLOUGH INN.' HOLFORD, Nr. BRIDGWATER, Som

A COMPOSITE POSTCARD of the Plough Inn. Made by Henry Hole in 1946.

A SPANISH TRAVELLER, who was murdered in his bed while staying there in 1555, is said to haunt the Plough Inn.

THE OLD COTTAGES at Kilton. The local schoolhouse was at No. 11.

A PASSENGER BUS stopping outside the Hood Arms at Kilve. These buses would carry passengers from Barnstaple to Bristol around the turn of the century.

CASTLE STREET, Nether Stowey, probably taken during the 1930s.

MR AND MRS CURTIS'S SHOP and post office on the corner of Lime Street and Castle Street. Taken about 1950.

NETHER STOWEY, looking over from Swaines Field, showing Butcher's Lane on the right. Probably taken around 1950.

COLERIDGE COTTAGE, Nether Stowey, c. 1910. Named after Samuel Taylor Coleridge who lived there from 1797 until 1800.

THE OLD MARKET CROSS at Nether Stowey, c. 1880.

THE OLD CLOCK HOUSE is on the left of this picture of Nether Stowey.

PLAINSFIELD, showing the Old Forge, which is now the Quantock Weavers. This photograph was taken during the 1920s.

STOCKLAND, showing Washers Farm on the right.

THE SMALL VILLAGE OF STOGURSEY was once a thriving town. As it declined, the old shops were adapted to private residences.

ST ANDREW'S WELL, Stogursey. The wells are on each side on the steps. The water from them is said to have medicinal value.

STOGURSEY WAR MEMORIAL, showing the parish church of St Andrew in the background.

THE HIGH STREET, Stogursey, showing the old baker's shop on the left. Probably photographed during the early 1930s.

THE DEDICATION of the Memorial Cross at Stogursey on 19 April 1920.

The Quantock Hills

THE BLUE BALL INN at Triscombe on the western slopes of the Quantock hills, photographed in the 1920s.

THE GENTLE, ALLURING LANDSCAPE around Courtway, showing Colliers Hill on the right.

COURTWAY, looking down from Colliers Hill.

A BRIDGE in the grounds of Crowcombe Court, built between 1725 and 1736 and considered to be a good example of a Jacobean construction.

A LOCAL FARMER POSING for the camera on his way to Crowcombe. This photograph was taken in around 1930.

CROWCOMBE, showing the Carew Arms on the left.

THE FORD AT LAWFORD, which is a small hamlet just off Crowcombe. This photograph was taken in around 1932.

THE THIRTEENTH-CENTURY STONE CROSS at Crowcombe.

FLAXPOOL, showing Flaxpool cottages on the right.

TELEPHONE WIRES, stretched and broken under the weight of ice during a very severe frost in 1947.

WHORTLEBERRY PICKERS on the Quantock hills, c. 1910. The wage for whortleberry pickers at that time was 4 d. per quart. The local schools would often have to close down as so many children were away on the hills picking the berries.

THORNECOMBE HOUSE, between Halsway Manor and Bicknoller. This photograph was taken during the 1920s.

WEACOMBE, which lies between St Audries and Bicknoller.

SECTION THREE

West of the Quantocks

CHILDREN POSING shyly for the camera on a sunny day in the pretty village of Bicknoller. Taken during the 1930s.

NEWTON FARM at Bicknoller. Walter was often asked by residents to take photographs of their houses.

THE NEW INN at Bicknoller. The poets Coleridge and Wordsworth would often walk over to Bicknoller from Nether Stowey.

GORES SQUARE at Bishops Lydeard, which was once described in an 1856 guide book as 'a village coloured blood red by the soil'.

BROMPTON RALPH. The church here has a fourteenth-century screen restored by an American in memory of his grandfather, who had lived in the parish.

COMBE FLOREY gets its name from the Floreys, who were the ancient owners of the manor. Combe Florey House dates from the eighteenth century and has an Elizabethan gatehouse.

COMBE SYDENHAM HOUSE was the home of Drake's wife Elizabeth Sydenham.

ELWORTHY lies above Stogumber and Williton. On the hill above is the overgrown earthwork known as Elworthy Barrows, not strictly burial mounds, but the remains of an iron-age camp.

MONKSILVER lies deep among the foothills of the Brendons. Elizabeth Conibeer and her two daughters lie buried in the churchyard, victims of the notorious Monksilver Murderer in the eighteenth century. The case was never solved, but some local people were aware of his identity. It was thought to have been a blood-letting ritual which went wrong. It is considered to be very unlucky to catch sight of the strange light which sometimes appears around the murder spot.

THE GIRL GUIDES outside Nettlecombe Court. This photograph is thought to have been taken somewhere between 1925 and 1930.

NETTLECOMBE COURT was granted to Hugh de Raleigh in the reign of Henry II and came to the Trevelyans by marriage in the fifteenth century. This photograph shows a meet of the Nettlecombe Harriers.

THERE IS A HOLY WELL at Roadwater, in the garden of an old cottage which was once a chapel dedicated to St Pancras. There is a mill, some pretty cottages and always the sound of fast-flowing water. The old mineral railway which ran from Brendon Hill down to Watchet passed through Roadwater. The railway closed in 1910 and the station has been converted to a private house.

THIS SHOP was once a post office, a bicycle shop and a bootmaker. It is now a private house.

THE ROADWATER INN is now a private dwelling.

THE INSPECTION of the Home Guard outside the White Horse Hotel, Stogumber.

THE HOME GUARD, with the special constables in the background, posing happily now the inspection is over.

THE RAILWAY HOTEL, Stogumber, was once famous for its ale brewed with water from a nearby spring which supposedly cured a man of leprosy.

MADDON HOUSE, Stogumber.

TEA ROOMS, Stogumber. The almshouses are just visible in the background.

COTTAGES, VILLAGE SHOP AND BLACKSMITHS, in Vellow. The blacksmiths has been converted into a local pottery and the shop is a private residence.

COTTAGES AT WOODFORD. This photograph is believed to have been taken at the turn of the century.

SECTION FOUR

The Brendon Hills

WATCHET DONKEYS bringing up limestone from the beach to one of the nearby lime kilns.

A TRUCK leaving the top of the Brendon Hill Incline. The trucks would go up and down the 1-in-4 gradient by means of a cable-worked device. The weight of the truck going down would pull up the empty truck.

THE BRENDON HILL INCLINE had to close in 1898 when the price of iron fell rapidly owing to the low cost of imported ore from Spain. This photograph shows its reopening.

BRENDON HILL MINES. In the nineteenth century, Welsh and Cornish miners were induced to come to the Brendons and houses, schools and chapels sprang up along the old trackway.

THE STEEP GRADIENT of the Brendon Hill Incline is clearly shown in this photograph. After the railway was finally closed in 1911 the sleepers were removed and taken to France for use as munitions in the First World War.

LUXBOROUGH, surrounded by numerous prehistoric barrows, sits high in a wild and lonely corner of the Brendon Hills.

THE RALEIGH'S CROSS HOTEL, taken around 1920. Originally a farmhouse, sheep sales were often held here.

TWO LATER PHOTOGRAPHS of the Raleigh's Cross Hotel, showing many changes.

RALEIGHS CROSS.

WALTER TOOK THIS PHOTOGRAPH of the Raleigh's Cross Hotel in 1926. His wife and two children, Mary and Henry, are posing in the foreground.

TREBOROUGH SLATE QUARRY, showing the waste tip in the foreground and the cutting shed behind. The quarry was worked by Sir Walter John Trevelyan of Nettlecombe Court.

INSIDE THE CUTTING SHED at Treborough slate quarry.

WORKMEN POSING for the camera at Treborough slate quarry.

TREBOROUGH is a very quiet little village now. There is a tiny nineteenth-century church only 50 feet long by 15 feet wide and a Bronze Age barrow on Treborough Common.

From Williton to Carhampton

BILBROOK, showing the baker's cart in front of an old timber house which has now been converted to stone.

TOMMY WILLIAMS'S GARAGE at Bilbrook. He was a well-known character in the village.

BILBROOK, taken around 1935.

RIVER COTTAGE, Bilbrook, probably taken at the end of the nineteenth century. The cottage on the left has long since disappeared.

STEPP'S FARM, Bilbrook, c. 1935.

APPLE ORCHARDS abound in Carhampton, and the age-old custom of wassailing the apple trees is still kept up. On 17 January, Old Twelfth Night Eve, the farmers and their friends gather in the orchards, sing old wassailing songs and hang toast soaked in cider from the branches. Cheers, singing and intermittent loud noises all add to the atmosphere and keep the tree spirits at bay, thus ensuring good cider crops.

THATCHED COTTAGES at Carhampton, c. 1920.

CARHAMPTON, probably taken around 1937.

THE DRAGON HOUSE at Washford was previously called the Green Dragon and licensed for Wesleyan preaching.

RESTORATION OF OLD CLEEVE CHURCH.
FEB. 1935.

THE INTERIOR RESTORATION of Old Cleeve church in February 1935.

ORCHARD WYNDHAM has been the seat of the Wyndham's since Sir John Wyndham settled there in the sixteenth century. The so-called Mother Shipton's tomb has a faked inscription to a Roman child.

SAMPFORD BRETT derives its name from the family of Bret. Simon Bret or Brito was a follower of the Conqueror and his eldest son Richard Brito was one of the four knights involved in the murder of Thomas à Becket.

MONKS STEPS, Washford. It was possible at one time to walk from here to Cleeve Abbey.

WASHFORD is a pretty village with its thatched cottages and flower-filled gardens.

CHILDREN AND ADULTS line up in fancy dress to pose for this photograph of the coronation celebrations of George VI.

THE WASHFORD CRICKET TEAM, taken in 1930.

BRIDGE STREET, Williton, showing the local baker making his deliveries. Bakers' carts of the type shown in this photograph were still in use up until 1938.

A LOCAL GATHERING outside the Egremont Hotel in Williton.

CELEBRATIONS of King George V's jubilee on 6 May 1935 are shown in these photographs.

DR KILLICK was photographed in Long Street, Williton. He was a very well-known and respected member of the community.

CELEBRATIONS of the coronation of King George VI. This was taken in Williton on 12 May 1937.

THE DEDICATION of the Legion Memorial on 9 July 1932. In remembrance to those killed in the First World War.

BANK STREET, Williton, showing Gliddons Agricultural Engineers and Workshop on the left.

BRADBEER'S GARAGE, Fore Street, Williton is now the Co-op supermarket.

LONG STREET, Williton, showing Miss Park's sweet shop on the left. Maybe the little girl was treated to some sweets after posing for this picture.

HERBERT'S SHOP after he made the alterations.

MOTHER SHIPTON'S CAFE in Williton.

BRADBEER'S GARAGE has been taken over by Somerset Motors in this later view of the corner on p. 80.

A LOT OF SNOW in Long Street, Williton in 1922.

SNOW IN BRIDGE STREET, Williton during the same year.

THIS SNOW SCENE shows the road leading up to St Peter's church in Williton.

A LATER VIEW of the road leading up to St Peter's church. Notice how the trees on the left have gone; probably pulled down in order to put up the electricity wires.

LONG STREET, Williton, after the 1922 snowfall.

WITHYCOMBE in a very old photograph, probably taken around the turn of the century.

A SUMMER'S DAY in Withycombe, taken at the same time as the previous photograph. It must have been a hot day, as all the windows are wide open.

Along the Coast

CAMPING COACHES at the Blue Anchor holiday park.

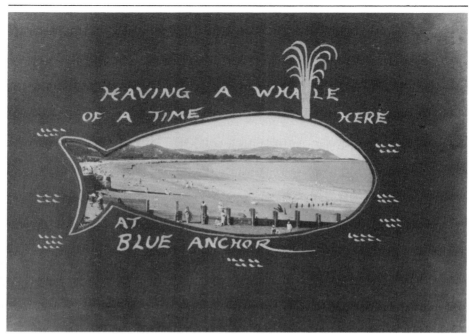

A PICTURE POSTCARD which Henry designed himself. It apparently sold very well.

A COMPOSITE PICTURE POSTCARD of Blue Anchor Bay.

THE RAILWAY CROSSING at Blue Anchor Bay. This photograph was taken sometime during the 1950s.

BLUE ANCHOR BAY, taken some time between 1954 and 1960. I wonder how many of these cars the reader can name.

THE BEECHES HOLIDAY SITE at Blue Anchor taken from the roof of the toilets – the only place from where Henry could get 'a good shot'.

CUMMIDGE was one of Somerset's three main ports in the fifteenth century, the others being Axwater and Minehead. It was the crossing place for early pilgrims and travellers from Combwich to Pawlett Hams. In 1480 a Combwich vessel, the *Anne*, sailed between Minehead and Bristol carrying fish, hides and cork. These days the small harbour of Combwich is used to bring material to Hinkley Point nuclear power station by sea.

DONIFORD BEACH, probably taken around the turn of the century. The shipway has been completely washed away now and the Donkey House has long since disappeared.

THESE PEOPLE on Doniford beach are quite likely to be collecting fossils. There were masses of various types of fossils (some 6 feet long) to be found between Blue Anchor and Watchet at one time, but sadly the beaches are empty of them now.

PADDLERS AND STROLLERS on the beach at Doniford.

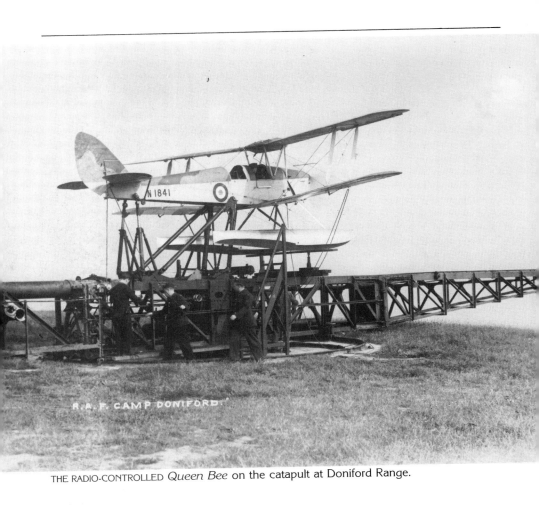

THE RADIO-CONTROLLED *Queen Bee* on the catapult at Doniford Range.

TERRITORIALS on manoeuvres at Doniford Range.

THE TERRITORIAL ARMY CAMP at Doniford.

LILSTOCK.

LILSTOCK was once the only harbour between the Parret and Watchet. It was originally built by the Ackland family and small sailing vessels would run cargoes of lime from there to Bridgwater. The Old Inn, which is shown in this photograph, catered for visitors and occasional seafarers.

TWO MORE RECENT PHOTOGRAPHS of Lilstock. The picture below was taken during the present day. Although mostly derelict now, a few stones still remain to remind us where the Old Inn used to stand.

LILSTOCK

IN THIS LOVELY OLD PICTURE children sit in front of the Old Inn at Lilstock, which in its heyday had a wooden pier with a summerhouse at the end where Sir Peregrine Ackland used to picnic with his friends. Today the pier has gone – swept away by a tidal wave they say; but the remains of the breakwater can still be traced on the beach.

SHURTON INN on a sunny day, taken at the turn of the century.

CHRISTMAS VIEW OF WATERFALL.

THE WATERFALL at St Audries Bay which almost totally froze up during the cold winter of 1947.

THE LOUNGE

THE POOL

THE BALLROOM   GREETINGS FROM ST. AUDRIES BAY HOLIDAY HAMLET   THE GAMES ROOM

A COMPOSITE POSTCARD of St Audries Bay holiday hamlet.

ST AUDRIES BAY.

HOLIDAY-MAKERS posing for the camera at St Audries Bay.

CHAPEL COTTAGES at Stolford. They used to be called Chipple Cottages by local people.

WARREN BAY CARAVAN PARK during the summer of 1953.

THE SMALL HOLIDAY TOWN of Watchet – a place of quaint nooks and corners gathered around the little harbour.

SWAINE STREET, Watchet, taken sometime during the 1950s.

TWO VIEWS OF WATCHET HARBOUR. The tidal harbour has an area of 10 acres and it is well sheltered from all winds with two piers and a breakwater; in its fine seaward approaches, the depth of water at its entrance, and its direct railway communications, Watchet harbour possesses advantages beyond any other small port in the Bristol Channel.

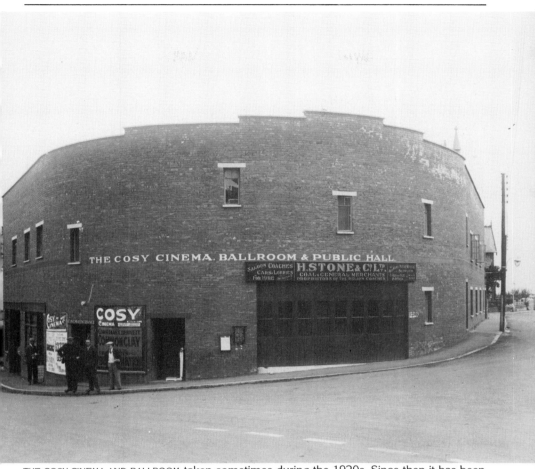

THE COSY CINEMA AND BALLROOM taken sometimes during the 1920s. Since then it has been converted into a shirt factory, a supermarket and a leisure centre.

THE *PONTYPOOL* outside Watchet shed, *c.* 1896.

THE DEER BRIDGE at St Audries had just been blown up before this photograph was taken. It had to be destroyed when double decker buses could not pass beneath it.

DISMAYED WORKMEN inside the Wansbrough paper-mill after a fire destroyed it in 1911.

THE EXTENT OF THE DAMAGE to the Wansbrough paper-mill after the fire is shown in these two photographs. It was rebuilt shortly afterwards.

Minehead and Dunster

ALCOMBE, looking towards Minehead. This photograph was taken around 1938.

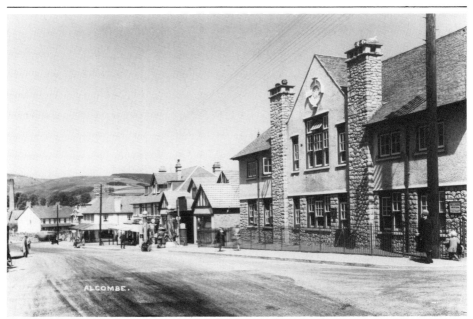

THE VILLAGE HALL, which was opened on 2 September 1925 by the Countess of Cromer, is on the right of this picture of Alcombe.

HAYFIELD ROAD, Alcombe, taken some time before the Second World War.

A CHARMING PICTURE of two people under an old oak tree, taken somewhere behind Dunster Castle, c. 1895.

DUNSTER, looking towards the Conegar Tower which was built as a folly in 1775. This view is from around 1897.

DUNSTER CASTLE MILL is an eighteenth-century mill built on the site of a previous mill which was mentioned in the Domesday Survey of 1086. It was restored to working order in 1979 and now belongs to the National Trust.

DUNSTER MARKET AND CATTLE SHOW, which was held on the first Friday in December, taken in 1907. It was considered to be a very important show for Devon cattle.

THE YARN MARKET at Dunster which was erected by George Luttrell in 1589. In 1646 it was pierced by a cannon ball and the hole it made in one of the beams can still be seen today.

THE MEET of the Devon and Somerset staghounds at the Dunster cattle fair on 2 September 1922.

DUNSTER.

THIS CURIOUS OLD BUILDING in Dunster is known as The Nunnery, but has no recorded history of ever having been one. It was used at one time as a guest house of the Benedictine priory and the basement is believed to have been used as a market trading house. Today it is a private dwelling.

THE RIVER AVILL which runs through Dunster and down to the sea is now silted up, but was once wide and deep enough for Dunster to be a port.

THE OLD PACKHORSE BRIDGE across the River Avill at Dunster leads the way to Gallox Hill, formerly known as Gallows Hill because two of Monmouth's men were hanged there by Judge Jeffreys.

CHALETS AND HAPPY CHILDREN on the beach at Dunster.

DUNSTER HIGH STREET photographed a little more recently than the previous pictures. It is heartening to see that little has changed except for the cars.

DUNSTER HIGH STREET, looking up towards the Castle, taken around 1950.

THE YARN MARKET is on the right and the Luttrell Arms on the left of this picture of Dunster High Street.

NORTH HILL, Minehead, taken in 1880, showing Quay Street and the beach in the foreground.

THE RAILWAY STATION at Minehead. The narrow-gauge line dates it to some time after 1901, but as there are still only a few houses on North Hill, this photograph is thought to have been taken before the First World War.

THE GREEN at Minehead, showing the Esplanade Hotel on the left.

THE PRIORY, Summerland Road, Minehead, is thought to be the oldest building in Minehead. It is now a greengrocers.

THE PARADE at Minehead, pre-1902. All the buildings in this photograph are still standing and are relatively unchanged.

THE PARADE at Minehead pre-1902, showing the old Market House on the left.

CHURCH STEPS, Minehead, c. 1896, showing Gunters tenement on the left which
was once the old workhouse.

THE MINEHEAD 'HOBBY HORSE' outside the Market Hotel. The custom is believed to date back to pagan times although its exact origins are not known.

THE BOOTEE, which is part of the hobby horse celebrations in Minehead. This photograph, taken in 1870, shows the poor man being 'banged' on the ground ten times before the hobby horse comes up and swishes him with its long rope tail.

THE UNVEILING of the war memorial on 19 November 1922.

MONSIEUR SALMET with his Blèriot monoplane on the beach at Minehead. These photographs were taken in 1912.

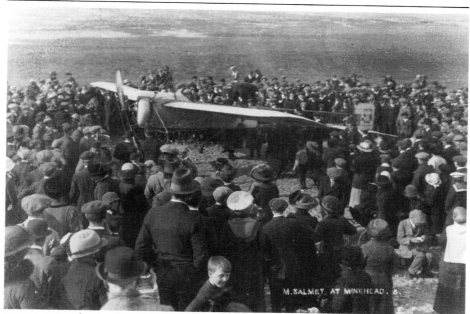

QUITE A CROWD has gathered around Monsieur Salmet, shown here on Minehead beach.

MONSIEUR SALMET took off, with his companion Herr Von Tromp, just after this photograph was taken at Minehead, but unfortunately they came down in the sea near Watchet and had to be rescued.

FROG STREET, Minehead, now renamed Holloway Street. The Queen's Head is still there.

THE OLD PRIORY in Minehead. This photograph was taken a little earlier than the previous picture.

SECTION EIGHT
Porlock and District

ALLERFORD in 1926.

ALLERFORD, with its fine walnut trees, lovely old cottages and packhorse bridge, has hardly changed since this photograph was taken.

THE PACKHORSE BRIDGE at Allerford.

A PICTURESQUE COTTAGE at Allerford.

BOSSINGTON. (22.)

THE CHARMING VILLAGE of Bossington has changed very little since the time of this photograph.

BOSSINGTON is also famous for its antique walnut trees and quaint old cottages. Not surprisingly, it has long been the haunt of artists and walkers.

ONE OF THE OLD WALNUT TREES for which Bossington is well known.

THE FARM at Bossington.

THE BEAUTIFUL LANDSCAPE around Bossington is shown to good effect in this view.

THE STAGECOACH leaving the Ship Inn at Porlock. The poet Southey sought refuge here in a storm and was so taken with the beauty of the area that he wrote a sonnet as he sat by the fireside:

Porlock! I shall forget thee not,
Here by the unwelcome rain confined,
But often shall hereafter call to mind,
How here, a patient prisoner, 'twas my lot
To wear the lonely, lingering close of day,
Making my sonnet by the alehouse fire,
Whilst idleness and solitude inspire
Dull rhymes to pass duller hours away.

THE WATER-MILL at Hawkcombe is still there, but no longer in use.

THE FAMOUS SHIP INN at Porlock, an old thatched building with the large round chimney frequently found in this part of West Somerset.

THE SHIP INN at Porlock Weir, not to be confused with the Ship Inn at Porlock, C. 1900.

WEST PORLOCK.

PICTURESQUE WHITEWASHED COTTAGES in West Porlock, which is situated between Porlock and Porlock Weir.

PORLOCK WEIR. The ancient port of Porlock, with its charming old cottages and delightful harbour, has kept its charm because of its remoteness.

AN OLD TRADING VESSEL at Porlock Weir, which operated at one time as a port.

A CLUSTER OF PICTURESQUE OLD COTTAGES at Porlock Weir. It was here the famous Porlock ghost appeared a week after the burial of 'a wicked boaster' called Lucott. Twelve persons were called upon to lay the ghost in Porlock church, but only one proved bold enough to tackle him. The ghost was finally laid by persuading him to enter a box, which was then hurled into the sea.

PORLOCK HILL, with its 1-in-4 gradient, has always been a test for vehicles and their drivers. This photograph shows the MCC trials competitors making their way up the hill in 1923.

THE BEAUTIFUL, RUGGED COASTLINE of this part of West Somerset is shown in this photograph.

SECTION NINE

Exmoor

THE OPENING MEET of the Devon and Somerset staghounds in Cloutsham in 1923.

CUTCOMBE.

THE EXMOOR VILLAGE OF CUTCOMBE is the highest in Somerset and contains many prehistoric remains including Cutcombe Barrow which lies about four miles to the south of the village.

DUNKERY BEACON is situated 1,707 feet high up on Exmoor. It used to be considered good luck to climb up there and watch the Easter Day sunrise. These two photographs show the cairn at the top of Dunkery Beacon.

JUBILEE. DUNKERY BEACON. MAY 6TH. 1935.

DUNKERY BEACON would often be lit to celebrate various occasions; in this case the jubilee of King George V in 1935.

THE SPLENDID VIEW from the top of Dunkery Beacon. It is believed that seven counties are visible with the naked eye.

THE VILLAGE OF HORNER, taken around 1930. Horner derives its name from *Hwmur* which is said to mean snorer.

THE PACKHORSE BRIDGE at Horner.

STONEY STREET, Luccombe, showing St Mary's church in the background. This picturesque, secluded little village was a particular delight to Coleridge and Wordsworth.

LUCCOMBE and the surrounding area has long been a delight to walkers and anyone who is interested in prehistory. The Iron Age field systems are shown on the Ordnance Survey maps.

THE CLAPPER BRIDGE OF TARR STEPS across the River Barle. The bridge is 180 feet long and is reputed to be the oldest bridge in England. During the Lynmouth flood disaster in 1952 many of the clappers were swept downstream. They were later recovered and replaced in their former positions.

WHEDDON CROSS is reputed to be the highest village on Exmoor. With its pretty thatched cottages, it has changed very little over the years.

CHILDREN POSING for the camera outside the village shop of R. Melhuish and Son.

WOOTTON COURTENAY lies among the steep hills at the foot of Dunkery Beacon. This photograph, showing the Rosemont Hotel on the left, was probably taken around 1935.

WOOTTON COURTENAY, taken from the Dunkery Beacon Hotel. It shows Dunkery Beacon in the distance and is believed to have been taken some time during the 1930s.

ACKNOWLEDGEMENTS

Grateful acknowledgement is made to the following for the help and information they supplied:

Mr Herbert H. Hole of Williton for his patience and tolerance in supplying most of the information needed for this book • Harry Nethercott of Roadwater for supplying information needed for many of the captions • Tom Ware of Nether Stowey for his invaluable memory in providing dates, facts and other relevant information • Joan Astell of Minehead for her kind assistance in providing a wealth of interesting facts about West Somerset • Somerset County Council museums service for their kind permission in allowing us to reproduce part of the Herbert Hole collection in their possession.

While most of the facts given in this book have been verified, apologies are given for any errors which may have occurred in the accuracy of information.